IWCS Workshop on Models for Modality Annotation

(MOMA 2015)

Held at the 11th International Conference on Computational Semantics (IWCS 2015)

London, United Kingdom
14 April 2015

ISBN: 978-1-5108-0227-8

Printed from e-media with permission by:

Curran Associates, Inc.
57 Morehouse Lane
Red Hook, NY 12571

Some format issues inherent in the e-media version may also appear in this print version.

Printed by Curran Associates, Inc. (2015)

Association for Computational Linguistics
209 N. Eighth Street
Stroudsburg, Pennsylvania 18360

Phone: 1-570-476-8006
Fax: 1-570-476-0860

acl@aclweb.org

Additional copies of this publication are available from:

Curran Associates, Inc.
57 Morehouse Lane
Red Hook, NY 12571 USA
Phone: 845-758-0400
Fax: 845-758-2634
Email: curran@proceedings.com
Web: www.proceedings.com

Workshop Chairs:

Malvina Nissim, University of Groningen
Paola Pietrandrea, University of Tours and CNRS LLL

Program Committee:

Johan van der Auwera, University of Antwerp
Delphine Battistelli, Paris 10 Nanterre
Anette Frank, Heidelberg University
Dylan Glynn, University of Paris 8
Ferdinand de Haan, Oracle Language Technology Group
Iris Hendrickx, University of Nijmegen
Caterina Mauri, University of Pavia
Marjorie McShane, Rensselaer Polytechnic Institute
Roser Morante, Vrije Universiteit Amsterdam
James Pustejovsky, Brandeis University
Andrea Sansò, University of Insubria
Roser Saurí, University Pompeu Fabra
Caroline Sporleder, Trier University
Veronika Vincze, University of Szeged

Round table contributors:

Ilse Depraetere, Université de Lille III
Elisa Ghia, Università per Stranieri di Siena
Paola Pietrandrea, University of Tours and CNRS LLL
Malvina Nissim, University of Groningen
Sapna Negi, National University of Ireland

Invited Speaker:

James Pustejovsky, Brandeis University:
Point of View: the Semantics of Perspective and Frame of Reference.

Abstract: The notion of "perspective" is employed in language to introduce a shift in the modal accessibility to a situation by an agent (speaker/hearer). When annotating different kinds of linguistically related phenomena, the specification language (markup scheme) usually reflects the needs of the immediate task. For example, in a spatial annotation task, such as traversing a landscape or following a path, distinct frames of reference must be distinguished in order to correctly interpret the language of viewpoint: e.g., to your left, north of the castle, in front of the pub. For personal or ideological viewpoint annotation, on the other hand, the scheme must reflect the ability to position a "view" relative to different agents. Similar remarks hold for temporal perspective annotation, and conceptual perspectives. In this talk, we explore a way of representing point of view over any domain, using a modal logic of perceptual knowledge. Among other consequences, relative frame of reference expressions are interpreted as the composition of relational statements about two objects relative to the agent. We show how this scheme can be used to annotate point of view in diverse domains.

Table of Contents

Preface

This slender volume contains the papers that were accepted for publication at the IWCS Workshop on Models for Modality Annotation (MOMA 2015), organised as a satellite event of the 11th International Conference on Computational Semantics (IWCS 2015) at the Queen Mary University of London, on April 14 2015.

The notion of modality involves a spectrum of phenomena that are pervasive in language but still far from being formalised. For an exhaustive formalisation, a joint effort by computational, corpus, and formal linguists as well as language typologists is required.

Computationally, the automatic identification and interpretation of modalised statements is a prime concern in a large number of applications, especially with the recent attention to opinion mining and social networks. Indeed, recent years have witnessed the development of annotation schemes and annotated corpora for different aspects of modality in different languages. While there have been efforts towards finding a common avenue for modality annotation, (the CoNLL-2010 Shared Task, ACL thematic workshops and a special issue of Computational Linguistics), the computational linguistics community is still far from having developed working, shared standards for converting modality-related issues into annotation categories.

In corpus linguistics studies of modality-related phenomena, researchers use an incremental method based on redefining categories after assessing agreement through several rounds of manual annotation, with the aim of finding the right balance between feasibility and expressivity of categories.

Formally, and from a comparative linguistics perspective, characterisations are sought of the range of modal types and their marking across the languages of the world, towards a complete classification of modal functions. This would yield a thorough understanding of the relations holding between modal categories, and an understanding of the grammatical vs. lexical nature of modal markers across languages. Insights from this tradition are crucial for the advancement of computational work on modality, since a comprehensive scheme for producing reliable annotated data must obviously be usable from a computational perspective, but it also has to rely on a solid theoretical base. In other words, a balance must be found between accuracy and detailing in the description of the phenomenon, and preventing proliferation of labels which might cause data to be too sparse to learn from, and also lower agreement among annotators.

Considered all of the above, the main aim behind the organisation of this workshop was bringing together researchers from the involved fields to join efforts in defining exhaustive and at the same time usable representations of modality, towards working, implementable annotation standards. Albeit small in number, the contributions that are published in this volume do indeed cover the topics we intended to touch upon, namely a general model of modality for a given language (Portuguese in this case), issue related to annotating specific modality phenomena, such as epistemic phrases in informal language, and, from a practical point of view, developing tools to support modality annotation, as *GraphAnno*. In addition to contributed papers, the workshop also features an invited talk by James Pustejovsky (Brandeis University) on reference and point of view, a round table discussing modality issues from several perspectives, including opinion mining, and a session devoted to actual planning future strategies towards shared standards in the annotation of modality.

The organisers
Malvina Nissim
Paola Pietrandrea

Models for Modality Annotation, MOMA 2015
Workshop Programme

Queen Mary University of London
London, UK

Tuesday, 14 April, 2015 — morning session

09:30 - 09:45	Get together, introductions, technicalities.
09:45 - 10:00	Opening. *Paola Pietrandrea and Malvina Nissim*
10:00 - 10:30	Towards a Unified Approach to Modality Annotation in Portuguese. *Luciana Beatrix Ávila, Amália Mendes, and Iris Hendrickx*
10:30 - 11:15	coffee break
11:15 - 11:45	A hedging annotation scheme focused on epistemic phrases for informal language. *Liliana Mamani Sanchez and Carl Vogel*
11:45 - 12:15	Annotating modals with GraphAnno, a configurable lightweight tool for multi-level annotation. *Volker Gast, Lennart Bierkandt, and Christoph Rzymski*
12:15 - 14:00	lunch

Tuesday, 14 April, 2015 — afternoon session

14:00 - 15:00	Invited Talk Point of View: the Semantics of Perspective and Frame of Reference. *James Pustejovsky, Brandeis University*
15:00 - 16:00	Round table: Modality from different perspectives. Planned contributors: – Ilse Depraetere *On the distribution of necessity modals in English: towards a multifactorial analysis* – Elisa Ghia, Malvina Nissim, and Paola Pietrandrea *The annotation of epistemic modality in spoken dialogues* – Sapna Negi *Automatic Detection of Subjunctive Mood for Opinion Mining Tasks*
16:00 - 16:30	coffee break
16:30-18:00	General Discussion *Joint modelling of modality annotation: state of affairs and future directions.*
19:00	Dinner

Towards a Unified Approach to Modality Annotation in Portuguese

Luciana Beatriz Ávila*†
Amália Mendes†
Iris Hendrickx **†

*Universidade Federal de Viçosa / Fapemig, Brazil
†Centro de Linguística da Universidade de Lisboa, Portugal
** Centre for Language Studies, Radboud University Nijmegen, The Netherlands

Abstract: This paper introduces the first efforts towards a common ground for modality annotation for Portuguese. We take into account two existing schemes for European and Brazilian Portuguese, already implemented to written texts, and to spontaneous speech data, respectively. We compare the two schemes, discuss their strengths and weaknesses, and, then, introduce our unifying proposal, pointing out the issues which seem to be already pacified and points that should be considered when the scheme starts to be implemented.

1. Introduction

The literature on the characterization of modality shows that there is no consensus on how to define and characterize this concept: modality can be taken as the expression of subjectivity, or as a distinction between realis and irrealis, or even as quantification over possible worlds, restricted by an accessibility relation. From a speaker's evaluation approach, Lyons (1977, p. 452) defines modality as "the speaker's opinion or attitude towards the proposition that the sentence expresses or the situation that the proposition describes". Modality involves thus "elements of meaning whose common denominator is the addition of a supplement or overlay of meaning to the most neutral semantic value of the proposition of an utterance, namely factual and declarative" (Bybee and Fleischman 1995, p. 2).

Logical tradition establishes three basic modal meanings: alethic, epistemic and deontic, related, respectively, to the notions of truth, knowledge and conduct. Following this tradition, linguistics takes into account the notions of necessity, possibility and obligation to define modal types. However, as well as there is no unanimously adopted definition of modality, there is also no consensus of which categories should be encompassed under the label "modal". In linguistic classical literature, studies organize in diverse ways the dimensions concerned to this phenomenon, depending on the theoretical frame. Among different approaches, the opposition epistemic and non-epistemic holds, and the values contrasted with the first vary considerably. For instance, Van der Auwera and Plungian (1998) distinguish participant-internal and participant-external modality and volition, evaluation, ability and capacity are other values considered (Palmer, 1986). Although most of the literature is centered on verbal expressions of modality (mostly semi-auxiliary verbs like may/might, should, can/could), studies on adverbs and modality have also been carried out for English. Several schemes for the annotation of modality have been proposed, mainly for English, and vary according to their objectives: some are strictly focused on modality while others are concerned with the identification of belief, subjectivity, factuality, as a source of data for applications in computational linguistics.

Our objective in this paper is to make a contrastive analysis of two modality schemes that have recently been developed and implemented for Portuguese, and to go a little further, by suggesting a standardization of these two proposals, to be soon implemented. We also consider that this proposal could be applied to other languages than Portuguese (regarding their particularities), given its broad scope to written and oral data. Indeed, although more modality schemes have become available in the recent years, their contrastive study is hampered by the diversity of modal values that are included, and so is the evaluation of tools for the automatic annotation of modality. The two schemes for Portuguese differ mainly in what concerns the text type that they apply to: the scheme proposed for European Portuguese (Hendrickx et al., 2012a; 2012b) has been designed and applied over written texts, while the scheme for Brazilian Portuguese targets spontaneous speech data (Ávila and Mello, 2013; Ávila, 2014). We will revise and compare the two schemes in section 3, report on their application to corpora in section 4 and attempt a unified perspective in section 5.

2. Related work

The growing interest on separating facts from speculations results from the importance of this task to NLP applications, as information extraction (Kartunnen and Zaennen, 2005); uncertainty modelling of clinical texts (Mowery et al., 2012); question answering (Saurí et al., 2006); classification of hedges (Medlock and Briscoe, 2007; Morante and Daelemans, 2009); and sentiment analysis (Wiebe et al., 2005).

Annotating modality, in order to allow its automatic recognition, includes identifying modal indexes, classifying them in a given typology (e.g. in epistemic and non-epistemic meanings), defining its source and its semantic scope. Many projects that have been developed for the annotation of modal expressions focus mostly on English and on modal auxiliaries. Some highlight the relationship between modality and negation (Morante and Sporleder, 2012; Baker et al., 2012), the annotation of modal verbs meanings (Ruppenhofer and Rehbein, 2012), or the construction of automatic taggers (Baker et al., 2010). There are also annotation efforts undertaken for other languages, such as the work on Chinese (Cui and Chi, 2013), European Portuguese (Hendrickx et al., 2012; Mendes et al., 2013), and Brazilian Portuguese spoken data (Ávila and Mello, 2013; Ávila, 2014).

Opposed to classical linguistic typologies of modality, these schemes describe in detail which elements in the text are actually involved in the expression of modality and their roles. These are the subject of the modality (source) and the elements in its scope (target/scope/focus). Other schemes (Baker et al., 2010; Matsuyoshi et al., 2010; Sauri et al., 2006) also determine the relation between sentences in text, identifying temporal and conditional relations between events or the evaluation of the degree of relevance of some information within a text, rather than classifying modal values. For more contrastive information on the existing annotation schemes, see an overview in Nissim et al. (2013).

3. Annotation schemes for Portuguese

While the modal scheme for EP has been designed and applied to written texts, the modal scheme for BP is designed for spontaneous speech, and it is more theoretically-oriented. Modality is taken in enunciative terms (Bally, 1932), that is, it stands for the point of view of a subject who evaluates the locutory material in a given utterance in a communicative act. The scheme follows the Language Into Act Theory (Cresti, 2000), which takes the utterance as its reference unit, and considers the scope of the modality to be the information unit (Tucci, 2007).

Both schemes converge in what concerns the elements that are not marked in the modal scheme, namely mood and tense. Nor do these schemes address factuality or a larger category of subjectivity and emotion. Due to their work on speech, Ávila and Mello (2013) and Ávila (2014) also distinguish modality, which is marked lexically and grammatically, from the pragmatic categories of illocution and attitude, which are carried by prosodic cues. As the three categories are often confused in their definition in the linguistic studies tradition, Mello and Raso (2011), through experimental investigation and observation of empirical data, suggest that modality is restricted to the semantic domain, although interrelated and projected into the pragmatic one. The same illocution can be modalized in different ways and performed with different attitudes, without affecting the illocutionary level.

EP (Hendrickx et al., 2012) combines a practical annotation with a theoretically-oriented perspective mainly based on the work of Van der Auwera and Plungian (1998). The scheme includes the values Epistemic, Deontic and Participant-internal, but differs in two fundamental aspects from the proposals of these two authors: Participant-external modality is not considered as an independent type, but rather as a subtype of deontic modality; and several other values are considered, namely Evaluation, Volition, and, following Baker et al. (2010), Effort and Success. The sub-values for Epistemic express the conceptualizer's perspective regarding the truth of the state of affair that is reported: Possibility, Knowledge, Belief, Doubt, Interrogative; the sub-values for Deontic modality express Obligation and Permission. The participant-internal modality has the sub-values Necessity and Capacity (internal necessity or internal capacity of the speaker, subject or other participant in the situation). Commissives and Evidentials are not annotated as a separate value but instead tagged, respectively, as a type of Deontic_obligation and Epistemic_belief (supported by evidence).

Declaratives are not included, and this is justified by the fact that they represent the unmarked level of modality (Oliveira, 1988), just as in the BP scheme.

The BP scheme (based on the latest revision of the guidelines in Ávila, 2014) considers a three-category scheme of Epistemic, Deontic and Dynamic modality, inspired by Palmer (1986). Epistemic modality carries seven sub-values: knowledge, belief, possibility, probability, necessity (here the conceptualizer presents what is said as a necessity, based on previous knowledge (*só pode ser doido* 'he can only be crazy, he has to be crazy)) and verification (the conceptualizer regards a state of affair as uncertain (*olha aí se nũ tem ninguém* 'check over there if there is no one'). Deontic modality encompasses four sub-values: obligation, permission, prohibition and necessity (the conceptualizer expresses his or someone elses needs). Finally, dynamic modality comprises the sub-values ability and volition/intention.

Table 1 presents a comparison of the modal values that are considered in the EP and the BP modal schemes: equivalent modal values (or sub-values) are presented in the same row, regardless of their designation. Both schemes are organized in terms of main and secondary modal values. The table also provides frequency of modal values in each corpus (see discussion in section 4). Most of the modal values are included in both schemes: it is the case of Epistemic_possibility, Epistemic_Knowledge, Epistemic_belief, Deontic_obligation, Deontic_Permission, Capacity/Ability, Volition. There are some cases of mismatch: the contexts tagged with the sub-value Epistemic_necessity in BP seem to be close to the value Deontic_obligation in EP; the Deontic_prohibition value in BP is most probably annotated as a Deontic_permission with negative polarity in EP; and Participant_internal_necessity in EP is covered by Deontic_necessity in BP (see arrows in Table 1). Two sub-values seem to have no equivalent: Epistemic_probability only occurs in BP and Epistemic_interrogative only occurs in EP. Besides those sub-values, three main values in the EP scheme are absent in BP: Evaluation, Effort and Success (there is however a partial equivalence for Success: when success is related to an internal capacity (e.g. verb *conseguir* 'achieve') it is tagged as Dynamic_ability in BP).

The EP and BP schemes share the same components and their approach is described as very similar to the OntoSem (McShane et al., 2005) annotation scheme for modality (Nirenburg and McShane, 2008). These are the main components: the **Trigger** is the lexical item that carries modality; the **Source of the modality** is the conceptualizer, i.e., the individual whose perspective and view point is being reported (this might be the speaker, the addressee, or another entity in the discourse); **Source of the event mention** is the producer of the text or the speaker; the **Target** is the expression in the scope of the trigger. The BP scheme also considers a Target-dependent component to encompass the cases in which the target, in a given utterance, is not explicit, but it can be recoverable in the referential chain of the text. The two different types of sources are marked up to capture cases where the conceptualizer of the modality is not the producer of the text or speech.

While the components of both schemes are practically the same, their conceptualization and application differ according to options in the delimitation of Trigger and Target and, mainly, to the text type which is annotated. For instance, the EP scheme follows a "min-max strategy" (Farkas et al., 2010) in which the Trigger is tagged as a single element whenever possible and the Target is tagged maximally (covering possible discontinuous sequences), while the BP scheme frequently selects multiword triggers. But the most significant difference falls on the Target component. The identification of the limits of the target is always a challenge, especially in what concerns consistency between annotators. In written texts the scope of the target is of a syntactic nature and the EP scheme specifies that syntactic boundaries should be respected. In spoken data, the target is in the scope of an information unit (IU) which may assume different functions: Comment (expresses the illocutionary force of the utterance), Topic (specifies the *locus* of application of the illocutionary force of the Comment), Parenthetical (expresses metalinguistic integration of the utterance) or Locutive Introducer (signals pragmatic suspension of the *hic et nunc* and introduces a meta-illocution). The BP scheme takes into account, for the annotation of the trigger and the target, the information unit in which they occur: Comment (COM), Topic (TOP), Parenthetical (PAR) or Locutive Introducer (INT). Example (1), taken from Ávila and Mello (2013), illustrates the differences in terms of target delimitation (for an explanation of the transcription symbols, refer to the authors' paper). The utterance in (1) comprises three different tone units, and the target of the trigger *tem que* 'has to/must', in the second unit, is *restringir também*. It leaves out the direct object of the verb *isso* because it is outside this information unit (defined prosodically). The same sequence in the EP scheme would take as target *restringir também isso*.

(1) é / [a <gente] [tem que]> <[restringir também] / isso> //
Yeah / we have to restrict too / this //

The EP scheme includes a polarity feature on the trigger and on the target that describes the polarity of both components and allows to deal with dual negation (Quaresma et al., 2014), and also a feature Ambiguity on the trigger component to describe cases where two or more modal values are valid in the context. The authors are conscious of the importance of dealing with negation and of the possibility to create an independent markup scheme for polarity, that interacts with the modality scheme (e.g. Morante, 2010) or to deal with both in a unified scheme (e.g. Baker et al., 2012). The approach taken leans towards the second option, although very tentatively. A specific study in the interaction between modal triggers and focus (the exclusive particle *só* 'only') was also addressed by the EP scheme (Mendes et al., 2013).

4. Application to corpora

The EP scheme has been applied to a corpus of 158.553 tokens, composed of 2000 sentences of written texts extracted from the written subpart of the Reference Corpus of Contemporary Portuguese (Généreux et al., 2012), a highly diverse corpus of 312 million words covering a large variety of textual genres and Portuguese varieties. A list of 40 Portuguese lemma verbs covering each modal value was the starting point for the extraction of the corpus sample and equal sets of single sentences for each modal type were randomly selected. Subsequently, the annotation covered all modal triggers found in the sentences. The BP scheme was applied to a sample from the C-ORAL-BRASIL I, an informal corpus of 139 texts, already published (Raso and Mello, 2012). The sample for modality annotation covers a sub-corpus of 20 texts with an average of 1,500 words each, thereby totally 31,318 words; 5,484 utterances and 9,825 tone units, divided into monologues, dialogues and conversations, distributed in familiar/private and public interactional contexts. The modal cues in both schemes are not restricted to modal auxiliaries, but rather take into consideration a large set of cues, such as propositional verbs, adverbs, adjectives, periphrastic forms and conditionals, and also nouns and interrogative clauses, in EP.

In both projects, the annotation was performed with the MMAX2 annotation software tool (Müller and Strube, 2006), which is free, platform-independent, written in java and produces stand-off annotation[1]. In the BP annotation, the identification of modal markers was manually undertaken by three annotators working independently and qualitatively validated through group discussions, and the files were later annotated in the MMAX2 tool with the full scheme by one single annotator. In EP, the annotation was done by one annotator and all difficult cases were discussed with a second annotator. A small inter-annotator agreement (IAA) using Kappa-statistic (Cohen, 1960) was conducted over the EP corpus, with 50 sentences and two annotators, resulted in a kappa value of 0.65 for the trigger and 0.85 for modal value (Hendrickx et al., 2012). A follow-up study on the identification of modal triggers in the context of an exclusive adverb was also the subject of an IAA that reported a higher score for trigger identification (0.85), a similar score for modal value (0.83) and included the target component, which attained a score of 0.64. These results are considered in line with those reported for English (Matsuyoshi et al., 2010).

In the set of 1946 sentences (158.553 tokens) of the EP corpus, 2377 triggers were tagged, while in the 20 texts sample of the BP corpus (31,318 words), 781 triggers were tagged with modality. The triggers of the EP corpus cover 2511 modal values due to 135 ambiguous cases, marked with more than one modal value.

The frequency of each modal value in both corpora is provided in Table 1. The comparison of the data is not straightforward. Several factors hinder frequency comparisons: first of all, the EP corpus was selected from a list of 40 modal verbs and even if the list tried to balance the verbs per modal value, the corpus is to a certain extent biased, as assumed by the authors; the set of modal

[1] http://mmax2.sourceforge.net/

values is not equivalent; the EP corpus is composed of written sentences, while the BP corpus includes speech transcriptions.

If nevertheless one attempts some initial comparison of these results, the most striking aspect is the significantly higher percentage of occurrence of the Epistemic main value in the BP corpus (not explained by the number of sub-values, but Mello et al., 2013, in a quantitative analysis, have demonstrated the tendency to the use of epistemic meaning in BP and pointed out that this value has a much higher association rate to different modal markers than the other two types, deontic and dynamic). If one excludes the three values that are not covered in the BP corpus, there would then be a total of 2123 occurrences of modal values in the EP corpus and the percentage of Epistemic value would then be 34,8%, still far from the percentage in the BP corpus. The analysis of this data would require a comparison of the list of lexical triggers considered in both corpora.

EP modal scheme	Freq.	%	BP modal scheme	Freq.	%
Epistemic	**739**	**29,4**	**Epistemic**	**506**	**64,7**
Possibility	279	11,1	Possibility	120	15,3
			Probability	24	3
[->Deontic]			Necessity	15	1,9
Knowledge	183	7,2	Knowledge	100	12,8
Belief	161	6,4	Belief	228	29,1
Doubt	29	1,1	Verification	14	1,7
Interrogative	87	3,4			
Deontic	**740**	**29,4**	**Deontic**	**189**	**24,1**
Obligation	581	23,1	Obligation	96	12,2
Permission	159	6,3	Permission	70	8,9
[-> Deontic perm., neg. polarity]			Prohibition	6	0,7
[->Internal necessity]			Necessity	17	2,1
Participant-internal	**248**	**9,8**	**Dynamic**	**86**	**11**
Necessity	126	5	[-> Deontic necessity]		
Capacity	122	4,8	Ability	17	2,1
Volition	**396**	**15,7**	Volition/Intention	69	8,8
Evaluation	**159**	**6,3**			
Effort	**110**	**4,3**	[-> Dynamic ability]		
Success	**119**	**4,7**	[-> Dynamic ability]		
Total	**2511**	**100**		**781**	**100**

Table 1: Modal values in the EP and the BP modal schemes and their frequency

5. A unifying proposal

The proliferation of annotation schemes for modality is certainly inevitable and the results of specific objectives of the different teams working on the topic. However, some attempt of standardization would certainly be of interest to the field, making contrastive studies an attainable goal. In the case of the EP and BP schemes, the objectives are quite similar and the properties of both varieties do not differ in what concerns the components of the schemes, although the list of lexical triggers might be variety-specific to a certain extent. However, any such approach should not ignore the specificities of each approach, related mostly to text type.

As mentioned in section 4, the set of components is practically identical in each scheme. The differences arise essentially in the list of modal values, the Target_dependent component and the trigger and target attributes. Let us start with the mismatches in modal values. We present in Table 2 our proposal for a unifying set of categories. Although the percentage of occurrence of the Epistemic_probability value is relatively low in the BP corpus, this value is nevertheless important in the modality typology and quite easily distinguishable from Epistemic_possibility. These two sub-values of Epistemic modality are covered by the lexical items *poder* 'might'/ *dever* 'should', *possível* 'possible' / *provável* 'probable', *possibilidade* 'possibility' / *probabilidade* 'probability'. Consequently, we keep this value in the final set. The uncertainty meaning conveyed by the Epistemic_verification value (BP) is in fact covered by the more general Epistemic_possibility value. The same is valid for Epistemic_doubt (EP), which translates into an Epistemic_possibility value with negative polarity (I doubt that this will happen ≈ maybe it is not possible that this will happen). Direct interrogative sentences are syntactically marked as such and their annotation as modal instances in the EP scheme involved marking the entire sentence as trigger and target, what seems unnecessary. Indirect interrogative sentences express a possibility value that can be captured as such in the scheme. Necessity is a concept that required further revision in both schemes: the EP scheme doesn't capture contexts where necessity is the result of circumstances (Circumstantial modality or Participant_external modality). In spite of the difficulty in establishing whether a necessity is external or instead is an obligation established by the entities involved in the state of affairs, it is by no doubt important to be able to distinguish the clear-cut cases. With this in mind, we keep the value Deontic_necessity (*é necessário que* 'it is necessary that'). We also keep the Participant-internal value instead of the equivalent Dynamic one (BP). However, we enlarge the sub-values of the Participant-internal category, so as to include several categories related to the expression of a subjective attitude of the subject. It is the case of Necessity, Ability and Volition, which is best captured as a subcategory. Since Effort and Success are types associated to the Participant-internal_ability sub-value, we decided to leave them out. Finally, we keep the category Evaluation, because it is interesting for studies of belief and opinion, although for this value we need more input and it should be revised in the future.

In what concerns the Target component, the difference lies in the type of segment which is tagged in the corpus: a syntactic phrase or any locutory material in the scope of an information unit. We consider that the functions of the information unit are the subject of a separate layer of annotation: the information structure. Also, the Target_dependent component is to be addressed in the co-reference level of annotation. Therefore, we keep the single Target component in the unified scheme.

The common core of the scheme is the list of components, the attributes of the trigger and the list of modal values. For studies in subjectivity and factuality, a special module would trigger a larger set of modal values such as Factual, Non Factual, Counterfactual.

Components	**Attributes**	
Trigger	Polarity	
	Ambiguity	
	Modal type	
	Modal values	*Modal sub-values*
	Epistemic	Possibility; Probability; Knowledge; Belief
	Deontic	Obligation; Permission; Necessity
	Participant-internal	Necessity; Ability; Volition
	Evaluation	
Target	Polarity	
Source of the modality		
Source of the event mention		

Table 2: Proposal of a unified scheme.

6. Conclusion

We have presented a contrastive study of two annotation schemes recently developed for two varieties of Portuguese: the European and the Brazilian ones. These two schemes have been applied to a written corpus of 2000 sentences in the case of European Portuguese, and to a sample of 20 texts from a corpus of spontaneous informal speech, in the case of the Brazilian scheme. Although they share the set of components to mark, they do differ in terms of the modal values that are included and the textual units over which to apply the scheme. It is important to stress out these two varieties do not differ significantly in terms of the system of modality, although differences are sure to appear in what concerns the list of lexical cues for modality, or the quantitative expression of the modal elements.

In this paper, we assessed to what extent the two schemes differ and what motivates these differences: we make a detailed comparison of the modal values that are considered by both schemes, explore mismatches, overlaps and inconsistencies, and propose a common ground that is rooted in a common concern in the field for some attempt to standardization. We suggest a common core for modality that would cover the list of components and a restricted list of modal values and specific modules that would apply according to the specific objectives of each task. We believe that such attempt is essential to conduct future contrastive studies between varieties of Portuguese.

Acknowledgments

This work was partially supported by FAPEMIG (PEE-00293-15) and FCT – Fundação para a Ciência e a Tecnologia, under project PEst-OE/LIN/UI0214/2013. The authors wish to thank the anonymous reviewers for their comments and suggestions.

References

Luciana Ávila. 2014. Modalidade em perspectiva: estudo baseado em corpus oral do português brasileiro. 253f. Thesis (PhD – Linguistics). Belo Horizonte, Universidade Federal de Minas Gerais.

Luciana Ávila and Heliana Mello. 2013. Challenges in modality annotation in a Brazilian Portuguese Spontaneous Speech Corpus, *Proceedings of IWCS 2013 WAMM Workshop on the Annotation of Modal Meaning in Natural Language*, March 19-20, 2013, Postdam, Germany.

Kathrin Baker, Michael Bloodgood, Bonnie Dorr, Nathaniel W. Filardo, Lori Levin, and Christine Piatko. 2010. A modality lexicon and its use in automatic tagging. In *Proceedings of LREC'10*, Valletta, Malta. ELRA, 1402-1407.

Kathrin Baker.; Bonnie Dorr.; Michael Bloodgood.; Chris Callison-Burch; Nathaniel W. Filardo; Christine Piatko; Lori Levin; S. Miller. 2012. Use of modality and negation in semantically-informed syntactic MT. Computational Linguistics, 38(2): 411-438.

Joan Bybee and Suzanne Fleischman. 1995. *Modality and grammar in discourse*. Amsterdam /Philadelphia: John Benjamins.

Jacob Cohen. 1960. A coefficient of agreement for nominal scales. *Educational and Psychological Measurement* 20 (1): 37–46.

Emanuella Cresti. 2000. *Corpus di italiano parlato*. Firenze: Accademia della Crusca.

Richárd Farkas, Veronika Vincze, György Móra, János Csirik, and György Szarvas. 2010. The CoNLL-2010 shared task: Learning to detect hedges and their scope in natural language text. In *Proceedings of the Fourteenth Conference on Computational Natural Language Learning*, ACL, 1-12.

Michel Généreux, Iris Hendrickx, and Amália Mendes. 2012. Introducing the Reference Corpus of Contemporary Portuguese On-Line". In *Proceedings of the Eighth International Conference on Language Resources and Evaluation* - LREC 2012, Istanbul, May 21-27, 2012, 2237-2244.

Iris Hendrickx, Amália Mendes, Silvia Mencarelli, and Agostinho Salgueiro. 2012a. *Modality Annotation Manual*, version 1.0. Centro de Linguística da Universidade de Lisboa, Lisboa, Portugal.

Iris Hendrickx, Amália Mendes, and Silvia Mencarelli. 2012b. Modality in Text: a Proposal for Corpus Annotation. In *Proceedings of the Eighth International Conference on Language Resources and Evaluation* - LREC 2012, Istanbul, May 21-27, 2012, 1805-1812.

John Lyons. 1977. Semantics. vol. 1. Cambridge: Cambridge University Press.

L. Karttunen and A. Zaenen. 2005. Veridicity. In: G. Katz; J. Pustejovsky, F. Schilder (eds.). *Dagstuhl seminar proceedings.* Annotating, extracting and reasoning about time and events. Dagstuhl, Germany.

Suguru Matsuyoshi, Megumi Eguchi, Chitose Sao, Koji Murakami, Kentaro Inui, and Yuji Matsumoto. 2010. Annotating event mentions in text with modality, focus, and source information.

In *Proceedings of the Seventh International Conference on Language Resources and Evaluation (LREC'10)*, Valletta, Malta. ELRA.

Marjorie McShane, Sergei Nirenburg, Stephen Beale, and Thomas O'Hara. 2005. Semantically rich human-aided machine annotation. In *Proceedings of the Workshop on Frontiers in Corpus Annotations II*: Pie in the Sky. ACL, 68-75.

Heliana Mello and Tommaso Raso. 2011. Illocution, modality, attitude: Different names for different categories. In: Heliana Mello, Alessandro Panunzi & Tommaso Raso(eds). Illocution, Modality, Attitude, Information Patterning and Speech Annotation. Firenze: FUP.

Heliana Mello, Flávio C. Coelho, Crysttian A. Paixão, Renato R. Souza. 2013. Distribution of modality markers in Brazilian Portuguese spontaneous speech. In: Quantitative Investigations in Theoretical Linguistics 5, 2013, Leuven. Proceedings QITL 5. Leuven: KU Leuven, 2013, p. 64-67.

B. Medlock and T. Briscoe. Weakly supervised learning for hedge classification in scientific literature. In: *Proceedings of the 45th Annual Meeting of the Association of Computational Linguistics*, Prague, Czech Republic, Association for Computational Linguistics, 2007, p. 992-999.

Amália Mendes, Iris Hendrickx, Agostinho Salgueiro, and Luciana Ávila. 2013. Annotating the Interaction between Modality and Focus: the case of exclusive particles. In *Proceedings of the 7th Linguistic Annotation Workshop & Interoperability with Discourse (LAW VII)*. Association for Computational Linguistics, Sofia, Bulgaria, August 8-9 2013, 228-237.

Roser Morante and Walter Daelemans. 2012. Annotating modality and negation for a machine reading evaluation. In: P. Forner; J. Karlgren; and C. Womser-Hacker (eds.). *CLEF 2012 Conference and Labs of the Evaluation Forum - Question Answering For Machine Reading Evaluation* (QA4MRE), Rome, Italy, 2012.

Roser Morante and Caroline Sporleder. 2012. Modality and Negation: An Introduction to the Special Issue, *Computational Linguistics*, 38:2.

D. L. Mowery, S. Velupillai, and W. W. Chapman. 2012. Medical diagnosis lost in translation – Analysis of uncertainty and negation expressions in English and Swedish clinical texts. In: *Proceedings of the 2012 Workshop on Biomedical Natural Language Processing* (BioNLP 2012), Montreal, Canada, Association for Computational Linguistics, p. 56-64.

Christoph Müller and Michael Strube. 2006. Multi-level annotation of linguistic data with MMAX2. In *Corpus Technology and Language Pedagogy: New Resources, New Tools, New Methods*, 197-214. Peter Lang.

Malvina Nissim, Paola Pietrandrea, Andrea Sansò, and Caterina Mauri. 2013. Cross-linguistic annotation of modality: a data-driven hierarchical model. In Harry Bunt (ed.) *Proceedings of the 9th Joint ISO - ACL SIGSEM Workshop on Interoperable Semantic Annotation* (isa-9), March 19-20, 2013, Postdam, Germany, 7-14.

Sergei Nirenburg and Marjorie McShane. 2008. Annotating modality. Technical report, University of Maryland, Baltimore County, March 19, 2008.

Y. Nitta. 2000. Ninshiki no modariti to sono shu^hen [Epistemic modality and its periphery]. In: Moriyama, T., Nitta, Y., Kudo^, h. (eds.), Modariti [Modality] (Nihongo no bunpo^3). Iwanami, Tokyo, 2000, p. 81-159.

Arja Nurmi. 2007. Employing and elaborating annotation for the study of modality. Available at: http://www.helsinki.fi/varieng/series/volumes/01/nurmi/. Last access: 21 dec. 2014.

Frank R. Palmer. 1986. *Mood and Modality*. Cambridge textbooks in linguistics. Cambridge University Press.

Tommaso Raso and Heliana Mello (eds.). 2012. *C-ORAL-BRASIL I*: Corpus de referência do português brasileiro falado informal e DVD multimedia. Belo Horizonte: Ed. UFMG, v. 1.

Josef Ruppenhofer and Ines Rehbein. 2012. Yes we can!? Annotating the senses of English modal verbs. In *Proceedings of the 8th International Conference on Language Resources and Evaluation (LREC)*, May 24-26, 2012, Istanbul, Turkey, 1538-1545.

Roser Saurí, Marc Verhagen, and James Pustejovsky. 2006. Annotating and recognizing event modality in text. In *Proceedings of the 19th International FLAIRS Conference*.

Ida Tucci. 2007. La modalità nel parlato spontaneo e il suo dominio de pertinenza. Una ricerca corpus-based (C-ORAL-ROM italiano). In: Actes du XXVe CILPR. (Innsbruk 3-8 September 2007).

Johan Van der Auwera and Vladimir A. Plungian. 1998. Modality's semantic map. *Linguistic Typology*, 2(1): 79-124.

A hedging annotation scheme focused on epistemic phrases for informal language

Liliana Mamani Sanchez
CNGL/Computational Linguistics Group
Center for Computing and Language Studies
School of Computer Science and Statistics
Trinity College Dublin,
The University of Dublin
Dublin 2, Ireland
mamanisl@tcd.ie

Carl Vogel
Computational Linguistics Group
Center for Computing and Language Studies
School of Computer Science and Statistics
Trinity College Dublin,
The University of Dublin
Dublin 2, Ireland
vogel@tcd.ie

Abstract

Most existing annotation schemes for hedging were created to aid in the automatic identification of hedges in formal language styles, such as used in scholarly prose. Language with informal tone, typical in much web content, poses a challenge and provides illuminating case studies for the analysis of the use of hedges. We have analysed conversations from a web forum and identified the manners individuals express hedging through expressions which differ slightly regarding to their lexical form from hedges used in formal writing. Based on these observations, we propose an annotation scheme composed of three main categories of hedges where the main class comprises first person epistemic expressions that explicitly note an individual's involvement in what they express. We provide here an overview of our insights obtained by annotating a dataset of web forum posts according to this scheme. These observations will be useful in the design of automatic methods for the detection of hedges in texts in informal language.

1 Introduction

This paper presents an annotation scheme for hedging focused on epistemic modality expressions in informal language. Hedges are used by a speaker to modulate the degree of commitment expressed by his or her statements. Hedging is deployed within various speaker states such as uncertainty, possibility, or politeness. A number of schemes have been proposed directly or indirectly to annotate hedges.

The elements involved in a hedging event occurring in a sentence are: the *hedging expression*, the *source* and *scope* of the hedge. The *source* refers to the entity experiencing or/and expressing the mental state represented by the hedge. The *scope* refers to the sentential constituents that are affected by a hedge expression. In (1), the hedges *might* and *may* are linked to their respective scopes. The source corresponding to both hedges, although only implicit in the sentence, is the sentence's author.

(1) These findings **might** [be chronic]$_{\text{SCOPE-OF-MIGHT}}$ and **may** [represent reactive airways disease.]$_{\text{SCOPE-OF-MAY}}$

Most existing annotation schemes label hedges as single units, while a minority have studied more complex classifications of hedges.

Bioscope is among the corpora which scheme is in the first group (Szarvas et al., 2008). Bioscope is a biomedical dataset of sentences from medical and biomedical articles tagged with speculation and negation information. Minimal units in a sentence are annotated as expressing hedging or negation, if such phenomena occur, and discuss cases where these lexical units are not actually used to imply speculation/negation. They noted that keywords differ in their propensity to be speculative depending on the domain. Ganter and Strube (2009) exploited the concept of "weasel word" in Wikipedia to semi-automatically build a dataset of hedges. Weasel words comprise expressions that Wikipedia editing policies discourage, such as *some people say*, *it is believed*, *many are of the opinion*, *most feel*, *research has shown*, etc. Vincze (2013) divided speculative cues in this Wikipedia dataset into three types: weasels, hedges and peacocks. Weasels signal uncertainty regarding an argument identity. For instance, the uncertainty in *some other* is caused by the lack of specification in 'While the Skyraider is not as iconic as **some other** aircraft... '. Hedges follow the regular conception limited to expressing uncertainty. Peacocks signal various sorts of subjective judgements such as *ardent* and *most distinguished*.

In the second group there are the works of Rubin et. al. (2010), Wiebe et al. (2005) and Hyland (1998), to mention few important ones. Rubin (2010) proposed a multi-dimensional certainty annotation model, where the main dimension qualifies expressions according to five categories that range from total uncertainty to total certainty. Wiebe et al. (2005); Wilson and Wiebe (2005) place speculation within a larger and more complex framework for annotation of opinions. This annotation was centred on the concept of Private States; i.e. they are not open to observation or verification, and they comprise opinions, beliefs, thoughts, feelings, emotions, goals, evaluations, and judgements and speculations. Hyland (1998) proposed a categorization taxonomy of hedges in scientific articles according to their function as: content-oriented, reader-oriented or writer-oriented.

We studied hedges in informal language in a dataset of web forum posts, but some issues emerged when attempting to annotate hedges according to conceptions in the aforementioned approaches. In Section 2, we provide an overall description of these issues. Our attempts to address these issues led us to propose a categorization scheme for hedges in language with informal tone which is described in Section 3. In Section 4, we present a summary of our findings from analysis and manual annotation in the dataset of forum posts, and in Section 5, we present our conclusions and views for future work.

2 Problem description

In this section we describe some issues related to the annotation of hedges in texts from an informal language type. The web forum from which posts were extracted belongs to a commercial software vendor; it is a forum in which users look to other users for advice in solving their software-related issues.

Most of annotation schemes mentioned in the previous section focus uniquely on the identification of a hedge and its scope in texts of formal tone and are only concerned with the interpretation of hedges as speculative signals. Automatic approaches for the identification of speculation (that implies automatic annotation of hedges) such as used by Light et al. (2004), Medlock and Briscoe (2007) and Farkas et al. (2010) follow the same line by targeting academic articles. Few approaches address annotation in informal register texts (Vincze et al. (2014) provide an exception). However, the informal texts of online web fora typically do not benefit from rounds of editing: the text is typically "noisy". Noisy text often contains ungrammatical language, misspellings, typos and non-linguistic strings (like emoticons), which limit the efficacy of natural language processing tools and methods (that perform moderately in well-formed text) when applied to texts with such informal language.

Despite acceptance that uncertainty expressed in a proposition is partly a product of reporting other points of view, as in (2), only few approaches such Rubin (2010), Wiebe et al. (2005) and Hendrickx et al. (2012) address the annotation of the hedging source, and none of the projects for automatic detection of hedges also address the detection of the hedging source. Disregard for the source follows from the fact that regardless of who the speculation experiencer is, a hedge is worth identifying since it points out to non-factual information.

(2) The existence of such an independent mechanism has also been **suggested** in mammals.

This approach can be thought of as 'content-centered'. Potentially, also identifying the experiencer of the hedging event could aid the building of the statements such as 'Individual A knows X and has certainty about it' or 'Individual B does not know whether X', and the like. This would be a 'user-centered' approach since explores the qualities and properties of a writer's utterances to find out whether a hedging expression reflects the writer's perspective or not.

In a domain of web forum posts generated by forum participants, the kind of expressions used to convey hedging are slightly different from hedges such as *suggest*, *potential*, *likely*, and *may* used frequently in more formal contexts. Informal expressions of hedging include phrasal expressions, acronyms and spoken-register transcriptions (e.g. *not sure*, *IMO* (*In My Opinion*), *AFAIK* (*As Far As I Know*), *dunno*). When the hedging experiencer is explicit in these sentences, this fact is lexically realized with the use of first person expressions such as *I am not sure*, *My opinion*, *IMO* or *to me, it looks like* in sentences (3), (4), (5) and (6) respectively.[1] These sentences convey the forum post writer's direct involvement in the hedging phenomenon, which is revealed by the use of 'I' as subject, the first-person possessor in *IMO* for 'In My Opinion', or by the pronoun *me*. This sort of phrasal hedges can also appear in a discontinuous manner in a sentence such as *I think* in (7).

(3) **I am not sure** which SP is on here, or how to check. Post: 18706

(4) **I'd suggest** the following additional steps: Post: 3655

(5) **IMO** it is best to always leave tamper protection on to prevent threats ··· Post: 16687

(6) **To me, it looks like** the O/P wants to try out the 2011 beta for testing ··· Post: 15134

I THINK

(7) **I** don't know how it's in other countries, but **think** it 's almost the same Post: 35934

Our research seeks insights that contribute in both content and user-centered studies of hedging. Therefore, our development of an annotation scheme and subsequent analysis take into account both perspectives. To this end, features the annotation scheme should consider are: a) identification of the hedging source, b) identification of the scope, c) domain-generality of annotated expressions, d) inclusion of different interpretations of hedging, e) functionality with noisy text, and d) capacity to annotate non-contiguous hedging elements in a sentence.

3 A scheme for hedging in informal language

The annotation scheme was built around three elements: Entities, Relations and Attributes. Entities are used to represent: a) a hedge, b) its source c) its scope, d) non-hedge and e) other discourse markers. Relations are used to link the hedge entities with their source or scope. Attributes are additional information about hedge entities that can be filled in during the annotation process.

We address three main types of hedges: a) Single-hedges, b) Not-Claiming-Knowledge epistemic phrases and c) Syntactic hedges. These are described in next sections. An additional label, "Non-hedge", marks entities that were deemed as potential hedges but not actually used in any hedging sense.

3.1 Single hedges

This hedge category corresponds to the traditional conception of hedges as single words conveying uncertainty. They are usually modal and lexical verbs expressing epistemic modality such as *may*, *appear* and *suggest*. The initial lexicon of single hedge instances considered for manual annotation were extracted from Rubin's (2010) work. Some lexical items such as "*can not know*" and "*don't understand*"

[1]The number preceded by 'Post' in examples throughout this paper corresponds to the post identification number for the forum post in the data set from which the example was extracted.

could overlap with Not-Claiming-Knowledge (NCK) epistemic phrases, but they are only deemed as NCK expressions if they are associated to a first person pronoun in the sentence.

3.2 Source

We define two categories of Source for a hedging expression: a) **Inner Epistemic Source** and b) **Outer Epistemic Source**. The Outer Epistemic Source is always the post's writer, as the writer selects a statement's content. The Inner Epistemic Source corresponds to the entity whose hedged point of view is expressed in the sentence; thus, the Inner Epistemic Source can be the writer or not. The use of *suggest* and *suggested* in examples (8) and (9), respectively, illustrates these two categories.

(8) USER1: [...] **I'd suggest** the following additional steps: ...

(9) USER2: User1 **suggested** following some steps, and you should consider [...]

In (8), USER1 is the one asserting his/her own hedged point of view. In this case, the Inner Epistemic Source is attributed to USER1, while in (9) it is attributed to USER1 despite the fact that USER2 is the proposition's author. In cases where the writer express his/her own point of view in the hedging event, the Outer Epistemic Source coincides with the Inner Epistemic Source as in (8).

When the Source is not explicit in the sentence, it can occur either implicitly as in (10) or as subject ellipsis as in (11).[2] Particularly, web forum text is prone to subject ellipsis due to its informal style.

(10) [...] *some sort of malware* **might** be preventing you from seeing the stock quotes.

(11) and $\epsilon_{subject}$ **don't know** if this is the correct place to ask it so pls lemme know if i shud ask elsewhere on the forum [...]

The implementation of the annotation scheme we describe here provides the means for marking the different cases when the Inner Epistemic Source is explicit or not.

3.3 Scope

In this research, scope annotation is mainly focused on the syntactic dependency head of the phrase affected by the hedge. This means that our approach to annotating the hedging scope is not as strict as it might be: at least the syntactic head of the scope has to be annotated and linked to the entity representing the corresponding hedging expression. This is mainly due to the inherent complexity of identifying a particular clause boundaries inside a sentence.

In our annotation scheme, the scope is separated from the hedging entity and linked to it by a SCOPE-OF relationship as in example (12). This has the advantage of avoiding the marking of extra words that do not belong to the scope. For instance for (12), Szarvas et al. (2008) by including the hedge 'possible' within the scope boundaries, tag *however* as part of the scope.[3]

SCOPE-OF-POSSIBLE

(12) Atelectasis in the right mid zone is, however, **possible**.

3.4 Epistemic phrases

This category includes first person epistemic phrases: they typically contain a first person subject, an epistemic verb such as such as *I think*, *I suppose* and *I wonder*, and a complement clause is embedded under the epistemic modality in this kind of phrase. In this section, we show how the concept of first person epistemic phrases moves away from the conceptualization of hedges coming from the epistemic modality tradition.

[2]Here, $\epsilon_{subject}$ is used to signal an unexpressed but interpreted subject.

[3]This is done to keep the hedge linked to its scope. This way of representing the relation was chosen because of limitations in the annotation tools they were using (Szarvas et al., 2008).

Early discussion about interpreting epistemic phrases as hedges originated in the analysis *I think*. Particularly, Thompson and Mulac (1991) consider this epistemic phrase has achieved a hedging state through a process of grammaticalization. Their view is that *I think* is roughly similar to *maybe* when used to express the degree of speaker commitment, thus comprising a grammatical sub-category of adverbs.

Scheibman (2001), Kärkkäinen (2010) and Wierzbicka (2006) showed that first person epistemic phrases used to express personal stance are highly frequent in various registers in contemporary English. They also describe particular properties of these phrases such as: a) representing the speaker's attitude with respect to the subsequent piece of discourse in contrast to when third person is used, there the piece of discourse is seen as a description (Scheibman, 2001), b) it comprises explicitly subjective claims in contrast to impersonal expressions where the hedging source is obscure (Hyland, 1998) , c) used to express knowledge states, as a boundary marker for turn-taking in conversation, a speaker's perspective marker, and as a way to align the speaker's with the listener's stance (Kärkkäinen, 2010). Besides, Wierzbicka (2006) suggests that this category of phrases merits recognition as a major grammatical and semantic class in modern English. She acknowledges a rigorous semantic and cultural contextual analysis of each type would be needed to provide an accurate interpretation, which she does in part.

A preliminary examination of hedge expression in our dataset showed that writers use first person singular epistemic phrases exhibiting characteristics mentioned above. Expressions of hedging such as *I'd suggest*, *I assumed*, *I am not sure* and *IMO* (*In My Opinion*) (see (14b), (15b), (3) and (16)) emphasize the writer's involvement in a proposition. In this aspect, they are different from epistemic phrases that have second and third person subjects as *They didn't know* in (13b). Annotating these expressions according to the traditional conceptualization of hedges would not capture the subjectivity expressed in epistemic phrases. This would result in annotating only the lexical verbs *suggest*, *assumed* in (14b) and (15b) in a similar manner as they would in (14a) and (15a); or in terms of epistemic phrases only *didn't know* would be annotated in (13a) which makes of this annotation equivalent to the one in (13b). The difference with epistemic modals is also relevant as they act as verbal modifiers, and even in first person subject propositions as in (18) the main constituent is the predicate they hedge. On the other hand, first person epistemic phrases are more subjective in the sense that the subject's involvement (revealed by the use of first person pronouns) is emphasized by the main constituent of these epistemic phrases (predicates related to mental states).[4]

(13) a. **I <u>didn't know</u>** what else to do and I still don't. Post: 288960

b. **They <u>didn't know</u>** the file and recommended to kill the process. Post: 4452

(14) a. ...and some researchers **suggest** that fibromyalgia and CFS are related.

b. **I'd suggest** the following additional steps: Post: 3655

(15) a. and it is **assumed** that he learned to read and write at the local parish school.

b. **I assumed** I would be able to retrieve all my files, but so far - no such luck. Post: 7492

(16) This is a kind censorship, **IMO**. Post: 171336

(17) <u>I for one **think**</u> the best course of action to take when you believe you are ... Post: 16687

(18) As I learn more about the problem <u>I **may** ask</u> for more info. Post: 25545

We believe first person epistemic phrases reach the same level of grammaticization as 'I think' showed by Thompson and Mulac (1991), so matching only the main lexical component expressing hedging would only partially represent the writer's commitment. The frequency and variety of epistemic phrases to be detailed in Section 4 support these intuitions. Furthermore, matching hedging expressions that resemble traditional hedges and that are not epistemic phrases is not always possible; that is the cases of *IMO* and *AFAIK*. Both acronyms reinforce our hypothesis that epistemic phrases are a distinctive grammaticalized category of hedges since they stand for the first-person epistemic phrases *In My Opinion* and *As Far As I Know* respectively, and even the case of *IDK* standing for *I don't know*.

[4]In Section 4 the main types of first person epistemic phrases are characterized according to their main constituent.

In some cases additional epistemic phrases modifiers modulate the intensity the subjective force, as in *I for one think* in (17).[5] However, we have not yet addressed degrees of certainty in hedging.

We reckon these expressions and the like constitute units of meaning with distinctive hedging qualities, and we aim to provide theoretical support to account for them as a newly grammaticized category of hedges. Ensuring that the writer is the one experiencing the mental state expressed by a hedge is highly relevant. One of the goals of this research is finding ways the epistemic source of a hedging event can be easily identified. We propose first person singular and plural epistemic phrases as hedge category when the subject of the epistemic experience is relevant to be identified. In Section 4 we provide overall description of our findings around these phrases that we call of Non-Claiming-Knowledge (NCK) epistemic phrases.

3.5 Syntactic hedges

Syntactic hedges constitute the third category of hedges we propose, given structural differences on the sentence level from Single-hedges and NCK hedges. We have considered in this study the classification of conditionals made by Iatridou (1991) (relevance, factual and hypothetical conditionals), and we have have applied tests proposed by her to manually identify which conditionals convey hedging. For instance, the writer is not expressing uncertainty in (19) about the interlocutor wanting to ask questions, but the speech act taking place is for making him or her aware that he would answer in case when further questions arise. The use of *if* in the previous example differs from its use in (20), where it helps to state a hypothesis.

(19) **If** you have any questions, feel free to ask.

(20) I'm curious what your system profile is, and **if** there is a potential incompatibility here.

In the annotation task at hand, it is not possible to have access to complete dialogue that takes place starting with a question, comment or announcement. Having access to the full text written where the conditional occurs might enable one to determine if this corresponds to the hypothetical type of conditional. Nonetheless, we have to acknowledge that the amount of effort involved on deciding about the speech act qualities of conditionals increases the time required by manual annotation.

4 Findings in annotation of hedges in a web forum dataset

Our annotation dataset was composed of 3,000 web forum posts, from which interrogative sentences, quotations and non-processable sentences[6] were dropped out, leaving a total of 16,720 sentences. To ease the manual annotation task, an initial set of hedge expressions was used to pre-annotate this dataset; however, the final set of hedging expressions surpassed in number and variety this initial set. In this dataset, we found 790 unique types of hedges, 272 of them belong to the Single hedge category, 300 to NCK phrases, 8 to Syntactic and 210 to miscellaneous hedges. In Table 1, we show some frequent types of Single hedges and NCK epistemic phrases.

Recall that we think the annotation scheme should be able to identify the stance of the author of annotated sentences. Thus, the first person pronouns *I*, *we*, *me* and possessive pronoun *my* were targeted to identify (NCK) epistemic phrases. We have classified these phrases in three categories: a) Primary epistemic phrases, b) Semantically extended epistemic phrases, and c) Lexically extended epistemic phrases. The annotation scheme does not exhaust this taxonomy, however these categories are relevant to give a characterization of epistemic phrases found in an informal domain style.

The Primary type of epistemic phrase are expressions composed of a subject and an epistemic lexical verb conveying speculation as a main verb. *I think* and *I hope* in Table 1 are some examples of this kind of phrases. In these examples, the main verb can be categorized as a Single-hedge; it could be identified by

[5] We are aware that *think* may have a non-speculative reading in this sentence.

[6] Non-processable sentences are mostly noisy text composed by non linguistic tokens.

Table 1: Frequency of hedge types for Single and NCK hedges[1] in the annotation dataset of posts.

Single hedges	Original	Freq.	Original	Freq.
	would	441	'd	48
	world	1	wuuld	1
	Normalized: would		Subtotal	491
	try	175	tried	147
	trying	111	tries	17
	Normalized (try)		Subtotal	450
	some	396	396	
	other	305	others	52
	Normalized (other)		Subtotal	357
	may	155	maybe	93
	may be	71		
	Normalized (may)		Subtotal	319
	suggested	49	suggests	5
	suggest	3	suggesting	3
	Normalized: suggest		Subtotal	60
	assuming	3	assume	2
	Normalized (assume)		Subtotal	5

NCK phrases	Original	Freq.	Original	Freq.
	i think	157	i thought	35
	i 'm thinking	6	i * think	5
	i thing	1	i was thinking	1
	still think	1	i am thinking	1
	i now think	1	think	1
	i thinh	1		
	Normalized (i think)		Subtotal	210
	i hope	59	hope	49
	i was hoping	4	i 'm hoping	3
	i sure hope	2	i do hope	2
	i just hope	2	i hoped	1
	i am hoping	1	i had hoped	1
	i am hopeful	1		
	Normalized (i hope)		Subtotal	125
	i do n't know	43	i dont know	8
	i do not know	8	do n't know	6
	i did n't know	5	did n't know	3
	Normalized (i do not know)		Subtotal	89[2]

[1] Lexical types such as *wuuld* and *i dont know* are provided verbatim. They reflect the variety of hedge types in the dataset.
[2] This is a condensed set of hedge types provided for the sake of brevity.

an algorithm aiming to detect hedging based on traditional hedges. The Semantically Extended epistemic phrase category contains phrases equivalent in meaning to the Primary types: the main lexical verb do not necessarily convey uncertainty, but as a whole the phrase conveys uncertainty, such as in *I don't know*. For instance, *know* is an epistemic verb but does not convey a sense of uncertainty and as it is not used for hedging. The negated counterparts of such verbs are equivalent to a primary type of epistemic verb conveying uncertainty as in (Holmes, 1988) – *not know* is categorized as an epistemic verb expressing epistemic modality. Nonetheless, we can easily see that negating *know* is quite versatile, e.g. *never/seldom/hardly/scarcely know*, *improbable (that) (personal pronoun) know(s)*, *hard to know*, etc. The same versatility can be thought of the case of *remember* and *see*. Informal contractions such as *dunno* are included in this category. To this category also belong objective epistemic phrases also known as non-factives (eg. *understand*) which do not presuppose the factivity of the embedded proposition.

The lexically extended epistemic phrase category includes phrases where the main epistemic component is not a verb, but the epistemic force is conveyed by another constituent such as a noun or adjective such as *I am hopeful* – see Table 1. Other NCK phrases are *AFAIK*, *IMO*, and *I am not sure*.

Some normalization techniques reduced the number of lexically extended epistemic phrases to primary type in the case of NCK, and in both Single and NCK categories normalization causes grouping of equivalent types; in Table 1 these groups and their normalized type are shown. Normalization strategies address a) standard and non-standard abbreviations, b) contractions, c) typographical errors and misspellings, d) tense and number variations, e) colloquial forms, and f) inclusion of modifiers. Single hedges were normalized from 272 to 189 types and NCK were normalized from 300 to 137. Some of these groups have particularly a broad range of types such as the group for *I do not know* which has 20 different lexical types of NCK epistemic phrases, including colloquial forms such as *dunno* and *donno*. We believe that these normalisation techniques and normalized groupings are useful to design strategies for the automatic detection of hedges in informal language styles.

Syntactic hedges comprise seven lexical types such as *if*, *or* and *when* composing a total of 1,307 occurrences.

A fourth category comprises miscellaneous hedges that could not be classified as any of the former categories. In this group, 314 occurrences are spread over 210 types ($\tilde{1}.5$ occurrences per type). They are expressions such as *fingers crossed*, numerical ranges and NCK-like phrases that are specifically related to the main discussion topic in the web forum such as *I am not a techie*, and *I am technically challenged*. We kept this kind of phrases aside because we wanted to ensure the set of NCK phrases is topic-neutral.

Regarding other annotated entities, we found that 3.57% (286 occurrences) of hedges have a source that is not the writer of the sentence where the hedge is used. Although minimal, this shows the existence of cases where the mental state expressed by a hedge use does not reflect the writer's one. Occurrences of hedges without scope associated to them such as *somebody* and *confusion* make up to 18.26% (1,496) of overall cases. Further analysis of these cases would be needed to determine if their presence in a sentence changes the value of certainty conveyed by it.

5 Concluding remarks

This paper presented an annotation scheme of hedges for informal language, where the main category is constituted by first person epistemic expressions (see Appendix A for a specification of the annotation scheme elements). We have shown that this kind of expressions has a distinctive character in the expression of hedging, different from hedges in form of epistemic modals and other hedges commonly used in texts that have a formal register. The variety of forms in these phrases reveals this is a relevant category of hedging in domains with informal registers, such as web fora. The expressions characterized here provide structures that can be exploited for the automatic identification of hedges in noisy text, where automatic deep grammatical characterisation is a tough problem. Distinctions between NCK phrases and epistemic phrases with subjects other than first person, and other classes of hedges in first person constructions were drawn. Both kind of distinctions focus on the writer's involvement in a hedging event.

We have proposed the annotation of scope in a way that sentence constituents unrelated to hedging can be excluded in annotation, which we believe contributes to the precision of scope annotation. There are many paths of future research, mainly, finding a way to assess the hedging quality of the expressions found so far by additional independent judges. This was not done this so far, because it requires specialized knowledge about the domain and because the annotation process has so far been exploratory in verifying whether Not-Claiming-Knowledge epistemic phrases are a prevailing category of hedges in the informal register used in web forums. Another path for further development is the automation of some techniques manually done so far in a way detection of hedges can be done in noisy texts.

6 Acknowledgements

This research is supported by the Science Foundation Ireland CNGL (Grant 07/CE/I1142) as part of the Centre for Next Generation Localisation (www.cngl.ie) at Trinity College Dublin and by the Trinity College Research Scholarship Program.

References

Farkas, R., V. Vincze, G. Mra, J. Csirik, and G. Szarvas (2010, July). The CoNLL-2010 Shared Task: Learning to Detect Hedges and their Scope in Natural Language Text. In *Proceedings of the Fourteenth Conference on Computational Natural Language Learning*, Uppsala, Sweden, pp. 1–12. ACL.

Ganter, V. and M. Strube (2009). Finding hedges by chasing weasels: Hedge detection using Wikipedia tags and shallow linguistic features. In *Proceedings of the ACL-IJCNLP 2009 Conference Short Papers*, Suntec, Singapore, pp. 173–176.

Hendrickx, I., A. Mendes, and S. Mencarelli (2012). Modality in text: a proposal for corpus annotation. In *Proceedings of the Eight International Conference on Language Resources and Evaluation (LREC'12)*, Istanbul, Turkey. European Language Resources Association (ELRA).

Holmes, J. (1988). Doubt and certainty in ESL textbooks. *Applied Linguistics 9*(1), 21–44.

Hyland, K. (1998). *Hedging in Scientific Research Articles.* Pragmatics & beyond. John Benjamins Publishing Company.

Iatridou, S. (1991). *Topics in Conditionals.* Ph. D. thesis, MIT, Cambridge, Massachusetts. Distributed by MIT Working Papers in Linguistics.

Kärkkäinen, E. (2010). Position and scope of epistemic phrases in planned and unplanned american english. In *New approaches to hedging*, pp. 207–241. Amsterdam: Elsevier.

Light, M., X. T. Qui, and P. Srinivasan (2004). The language of bioscience: Facts, speculations, and statements in between. *Proceedings of BioLink 2004 Workshop on Linking Biological Literature, Ontologies and Databases: Tools for Users*, 17 – 24.

Medlock, B. and T. Briscoe (2007). Weakly supervised learning for hedge classification in scientific literature. In *Proceedings of the 45th Annual Meeting of the Association of Computational Linguistics*, Prague, Czech Republic, pp. 992–999.

Rubin, V. L. (2010). Epistemic modality: From uncertainty to certainty in the context of information seeking as interactions with texts. *Information Processing & Management 46*(5), 533–540.

Scheibman, J. (2001). Local patterns of subjectivity in person and verb type in. In J. L. Bybee and P. Hopper (Eds.), *Frequency and the Emergence of Linguistic Structure*, Volume 45 of *Typological studies in language*, pp. 61–89. Amsterdam; Philadelphia: John Benjamins Publishing Company.

Szarvas, G., V. Vincze, R. Farkas, and J. Csirik (2008). The BioScope corpus: annotation for negation, uncertainty and their scope in biomedical texts. In *Proceedings of the Workshop on Current Trends in Biomedical Natural Language Processing*, Columbus, Ohio, pp. 38–45.

Thompson, S. A. and A. Mulac (1991). A quantitative perspective on the grammaticization of epistemic parentheticals in english. In *Approaches to Grammaticalization*, pp. 314–329. John Benjamins.

Vincze, V. (2013, October). Weasels, hedges and peacocks: Discourse-level uncertainty in wikipedia articles. In *Proceedings of the Sixth International Joint Conference on Natural Language Processing*, Nagoya, Japan, pp. 383–391. Asian Federation of Natural Language Processing.

Vincze, V., I. K. Simkó, and V. Varga (2014). *Proceedings of LAW VIII - The 8th Linguistic Annotation Workshop*, Chapter Annotating Uncertainty in Hungarian Webtext, pp. 64–69. Association for Computational Linguistics and Dublin City University.

Vincze, V., G. Szarvas, R. Farkas, G. Mora, and J. Csirik (2008). The BioScope corpus: biomedical texts annotated for uncertainty, negation and their scopes. *BMC Bioinformatics 9*(Suppl 11), S9.

Wiebe, J., T. Wilson, and C. Cardie (2005). Annotating expressions of opinions and emotions in language ANN. *Language Resources and Evaluation 39*(2/3), 164–210.

Wierzbicka, A. (2006). *English: meaning and culture.* Oxford University Press, USA.

Wilson, T. and J. Wiebe (2005). Annotating attributions and private states. In *Proceedings of the Workshop on Frontiers in Corpus Annotations II: Pie in the Sky*, CorpusAnno'05, Stroudsburg, PA, USA, pp. 53–60. ACL.

Appendix A Annotation scheme syntax

```
<entity> => <hedge> | <non-hedge> | <scope>| <source>
<hedge> => <single> | <not-claiming-knowledge> | <syntactic> | <miscellaneous>
<relations> => <source-of> | <scope-is>
<attribute> => <inner-epistemic-source>
<inner-epistemic-source> => writer | other

<has-attribute> => (<hedge>,<attribute>)
<source-of> => (<hedge>,<source>)
<scope-is> =>(<hedge>,<scope>)
```

Annotating modals with GraphAnno, a configurable lightweight tool for multi-level annotation

Volker Gast
Friedrich Schiller University Jena
volker.gast@uni-jena.de

Lennart Bierkandt
Friedrich Schiller University Jena
post@lennartbierkandt.de

Christoph Rzymski
Friedrich Schiller University Jena
christoph.rzymski@uni-jena.de

1 Introduction

GraphAnno is a configurable tool for multi-level annotation which caters for the entire workflow from corpus import to data export and thus provides a suitable environment for the manual annotation of modals in their sentential contexts. Given its generic data model, it is particularly suitable for enriching existing corpora, e.g. by adding semantic annotations to syntactic ones. In this contribution, we present the functionalities of GraphAnno and make a concrete proposal for the treatment of modals in a corpus, with a focus on scope interactions. We have nothing to say about the specific categories to be annotated. Its generic design allows GraphAnno to be used with various annotation schemes, like those proposed by Hendrickx et al. (2012), Nissim et al. (2013) and Rubinstein et al. (2013). We will use generic category labels from theoretical linguistics for illustration purposes.

After providing some background information on the tool in Section 2 we show how GraphAnno deals with four major tasks of corpus-based projects, i.e., corpus import (Section 3), annotation (Section 4), searching (Section 5) and data export (Section 6).

2 Some background on GraphAnno

GraphAnno was originally designed as a lightweight prototype for a more powerful multi-level annotation tool, Atomic (cf. Druskat et al. 2014), in a project on multi-level annotation of cross-linguistic data.[1] The focus was thus on functionality, rather than, for instance, performance with large data sets. The tool has been used in various corpus-based projects (e.g. Gast 2015), and it has proven a stable and user-friendly application, specifically for small-scale annotation projects. GraphAnno was therefore published in 2014, and will continue to be maintained.[2]

GraphAnno is so called because the corpus data is programme-internally represented, and also visually displayed, as a graph, consisting of annotated nodes and edges. Given its generic data model, it can handle any type of graph structure, not only trees. Annotations can be restricted and controlled with dictionaries of attribute-value pairs.

The application requires Graphviz[3] and Ruby.[4] It handles dependencies on other libraries using the RubyGems package manager. It is platform-independent, and an exe-file for easy use on a Windows system is available, bundling the required Ruby runtime environment. The tool has a browser-based interface. To get going, the user starts a ruby process (by double click or from a command line) and accesses the annotation projects by visiting the URL 'http://localhost:4567'.

---

[1] LinkType, sponsored by the German Science Foundation (DFG, grant GA-1288/5). Financial support from this institution is gratefully acknowledged; see also http://www.linktype.iaa.uni-jena.de. [2] https://github.com/LBierkandt/graph-anno
[3] http://www.graphviz.org [4] http://www.ruby-lang.org

GraphAnno is operated via a command line at the bottom of the browser window. Annotations are created with one-letter commands such as `n` (create a node), `g` (groupe nodes into constituents), `e` (create an edge), `d` (delete nodes/edges) and `a` (annotation of attribute-value pairs; see below for examples). For navigation in the corpus and the choice of an annotation level, there are dropdown fields, and the tool comes with some key bindings giving access to its most important functionalities, e.g. for zooming and navigation. Some important functions are controlled with the function keys F6 (filter), F7 (search), F8 (configuration) and F9 (metadata). In the configurations window, users can, most importantly, define annotation levels and set some parameters concerning matters of visual representation (e.g. colours for annotation levels and highlighting), as well as define shortcuts and store search macros (cf. Section 5).

Unlike Atomic, which is part of the ANNIS-infrastructure,[5] GraphAnno is intended to be 'promiscuous', with interoperability being achieved via Python[6] and NLTK.[7] An important feature exhibited by GraphAnno which is not (yet) available for Atomic is the search and export functions (cf. Sects. 5 and 6). GraphAnno is thus designed for smaller projects and exploratory studies, as it allows users to analyse and inspect the data during the process of annotation. It is distinguished from other tools such as MMAX2[8] and Exmaralda[9] by its focus on hierarchical multi-level annotation with (online) 2D-visualization, and from generic graph tools such as Cytospace[10] by its specifically linguistic functionalities.

3 Corpus import

Corpora can be imported with the command `import` in the command line, which opens a dialogue window. They can either be loaded from a text file, or be pasted into a text field. For preprocessing, punkt segmenters for eleven languages are integrated and can be selected. A corpus format can also be specified using regular expressions. More richly annotated corpora, especially treebanks, can be imported via Python and NLTK. GraphAnno natively uses JSON-files for persistent storing. For the import of treebanks (e.g. the Penn Treebank)[11] and of more specific resources like the the BioScope corpus[12] (Vincze et al. 2008) converters are available. Being connected to the NLTK infrastructure already, an even closer integration is envisaged for the near future. Converted annotation projects are read into GraphAnno with the `load`-command, like any other project created with GraphAnno itself.

Figure 1 shows a structural representation of the sentence in (1), imported from the Penn Treebank. The sentence is displayed as a graph as well as in plain text at the bottom of the window.

(1) These individuals may not necessarily be under investigation when they hire lawyers.

The sentence in (2), imported from the BioScope corpus, is shown in GraphAnno-format in Figure 2 (for reasons of space, only the part wih a modal is displayed).

(2)
```
<sentence id="S177.8">
   Oxidative stress obtained by the addition of H2O2 to the
   culture medium of J.Jhan or U937 cells
   <xcope id="X177.8.2">
      <cue type="speculation" ref="X177.8.2">could</cue>
      <xcope id="X177.8.1">
         <cue type="negation" ref="X177.8.1">not</cue>
         by itself induce NF-kappa B activation
      </xcope>
    </xcope>.
</sentence>
```

While the BioScope corpus, as well as most annotation schemes for modals (e.g. Hendrickx et al. 2012; Nissim et al. 2013; Rubinstein et al. 2013), works at a single (structural) level of annotation, even though the annotations are (partly) semantic in nature, GraphAnno is a multi-level annotation tool and allows us

---

[5] http://annis-tools.org/ [6] https://www.python.org/ [7] http://www.nltk.org [8] http://mmax2.sourceforge.net/
[9] http://www.exmaralda.org/en [10] http://www.cytoscape.org/ [11] http://www.cis.upenn.edu/~treebank/
[12] http://rgai.inf.u-szeged.hu/bioscope

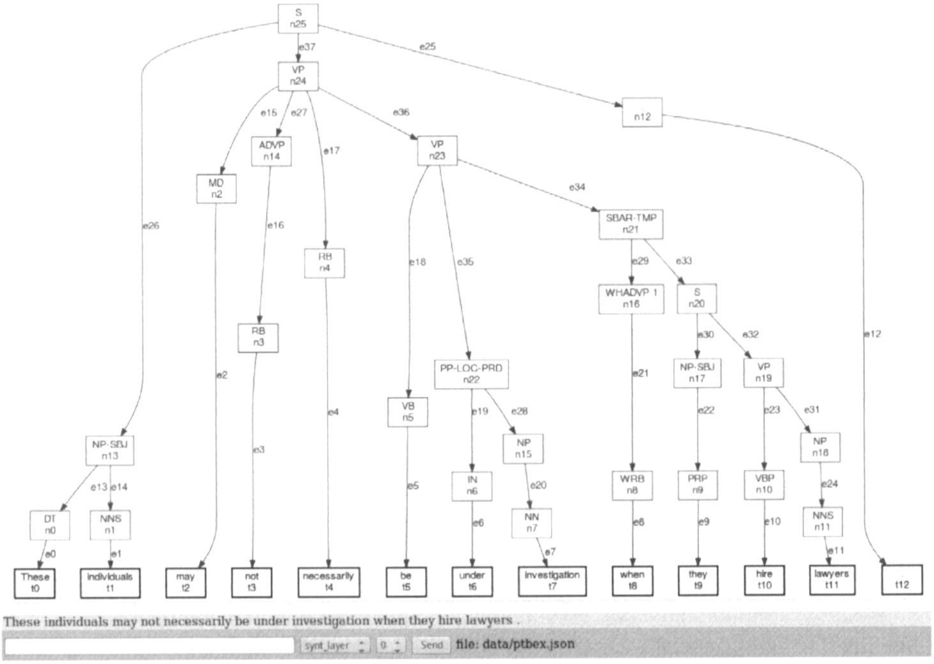

Figure 1: A structurally annotated sentence in GraphAnno

to distinguish between a structural and a semantic layer. We argue that properties of semantic entities should be attributed to, i.e., annotated on, elements specifically representing meaning, not structure. Moreover, the advantage of multi-level annotation is that it allows us to add semantic annotations to existing structural ones – to *enrich* corpora, rather than annotating from scratch. We believe that by combining structural with semantic annotations, we can gain information that is potentially useful for machine learning. In what follows, we use syntactic structures as our point of departure and add manual annotations, which we consider a reasonable workflow for small-scale annotation projects.

4 Annotating modals manually

Having imported a corpus, it can be (further) annotated at a theoretically infinite number of levels. The levels are visually distinguished by colours, but they can also be separated by hiding specific levels, or filtering them out (cf. below). The structural level ('s-layer'), as displayed in Figure 1, is by default blue.

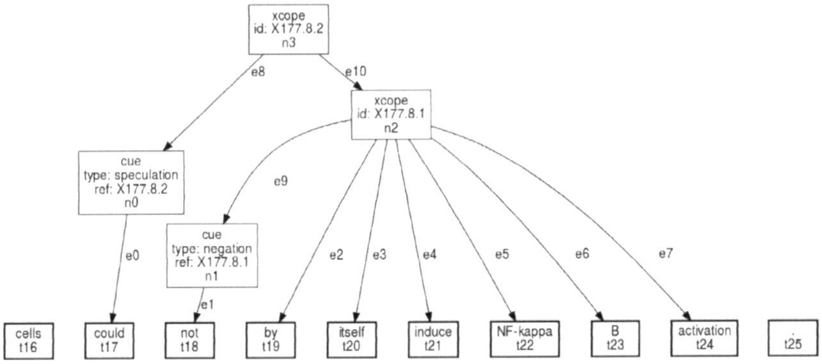

Figure 2: A sentence imported from the BioScope corpus

4.1 Creating semantic structure

For a corpus-based study of modality, the annotation of scope relations is a central concern – for instance, because they interact systematically with the reading of a given modal (cf. von Fintel 2006 for a theoretical overview). For (1) above we can assume the simplified semantic representation shown in (3):

(3) MAY [NOT [NEC [these individuals BE under investigation . . .]]]

As has been mentioned, GraphAnno allows for a free configuration of levels, including a free choice of names and colours, but it comes by default with two levels, the 's(tructural)-layer' as represented in Figure 1 above, and the 'f(unctional)-layer'. We will use the functional layer for our semantic annotations. The annotation level can be selected from the dropdown field next to the command line, or in the command line itself. Users can also choose to assign annotations to both levels by selecting the 'fs-layer'. Note that annotations belonging to different levels can be searched together. Technically, they belong to the same graph. Assigning a given annotation to one level or another is thus often a theoretical decision and does not have any far-reaching practical consequences.

Scope relations holding between scope-bearing operators can be indicated by grouping the (denotations of the) constituents as shown in (3) on the semantic level (f-layer). In some but not all cases, the relevant structures are also represented syntactically, so that we can work on the fs-level. In a first step, we can create a node corresponding to the inner proposition 'These individuals BE under investigation . . . '. For this purpose, we can assign the NP 'these individuals' and the VP 'BE under investigation . . . ' to the f-layer (they belong to the s-layer already). Membership to a given level is stored as an attribute-value pair, with the name of the level as the attribute, and either `t` or `f` as the value, but the level can be specified with a simple shortcut like `f`, too. Annotations can be assigned to several elements at the same time. For example, the nodes `n2`, `n3` and `n4` can be assigned to the semantic level as is shown in (4) (`a` is the command for 'annotate').

(4) `a n2 n3 n4 f`

Having assigned the nodes `n2`, `n3` and `n4` to the f-layer, we can create a parent node dominating them. Parent nodes are created with the command `g` (for 'group'), followed by the identifiers of the nodes, and any attribute-value pairs. A node corresponding to the proposition 'these individuals BE under investigation . . . ' is created as is shown in (5) (the type *t* (Russell 1908) is assigned to the newly created node).

(5) `g n13 n23 cat:t`

We can now create successively higher-level nodes of type *t*, moving leftwards in the representation in (3) above. Inevitably in multi-level annotation, such annotations will lead to complex tree diagrams, and for users this may quickly become confusing. GraphAnno therefore allows users to hide or filter the graph (with F6). 'Hiding' means representing the hidden part in light grey, thus allowing for an inspection of the whole graph with visual emphasis on relevant parts – see Figure 3, where all elements not belonging to the semantic level are hidden. The resulting graph is still complex, but the different

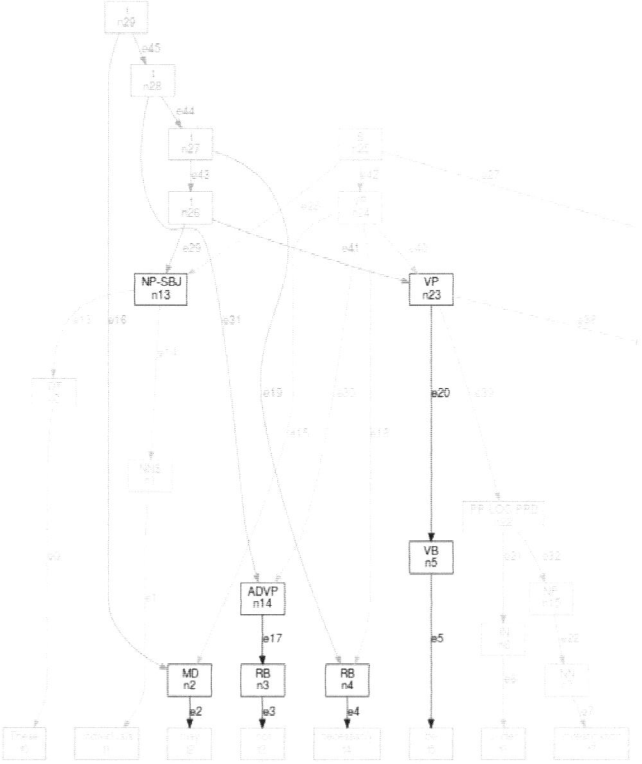

Figure 3: Hiding the structural level

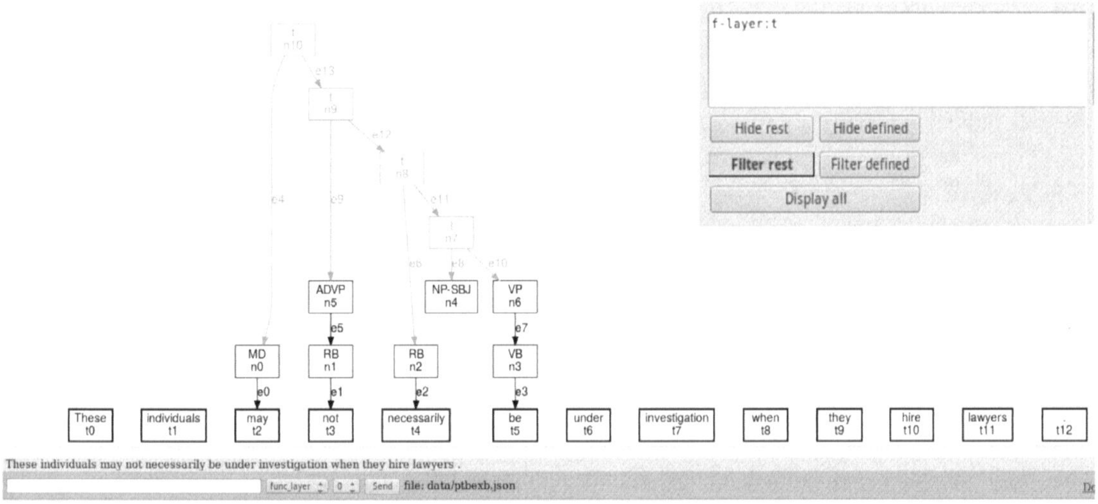

Figure 4: Filtering the structural level

colours allow for a reasonably clear visual differentiation. When working on an annotation project, it is often more convenient to not just hide specific parts of a tree diagram, but to filter them out, i.e., to have GraphAnno display a new graph with only those portions of the graph that are currently relevant. It is important to note that the full structure of the graph is preserved, e.g. for search procedures; it is not represented visually, however.

Figure 4 shows the result of filtering out all those elements that are not represented at the semantic level. The small window in the top-right corner contains the filter criterion, here `f-layer:t`, and the graph shown in Figure 4 was generated be pressing 'Filter rest'. Note that node `n4`, corresponding to the subject 'these individuals', appears to be dangling, but is actually linked to tokens `t0` and `t1` at the structural level.

In example (1), the order of elements mirrors their relative scope relations, and the graph is therefore relatively homogeneous in terms of its branching direction. An example of a modal being in the scope of negation (and thus leading to crossing edges) is shown in Figure 5. As the portion of the Penn Treebank that is accessible via NLTK does not contain an example of this type with *may*, we are using the made-up example *You may not go*. Note that node `n0`, corresponding to the pronoun *you*, is not linked to its token, as the corresponding edge has not been assigned to the f-layer.

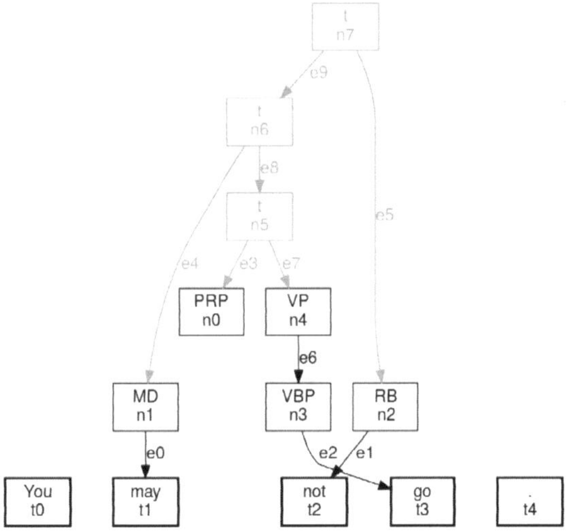

Figure 5: A deontic modal in the scope of negation

4.2 Towards a richer annotation of modality

So far, we have only attributed properties to elements of a graph (nodes and edges) that are not explicitly shown in the graph. This applies to category labels and layer specifications. In this way, we have indicated scope relations holding between semantic elements that are tied to syntactic elements without receiving any annotations of their own. We can now enrich the graphs with semantic annotations. GraphAnno allows the user to assign any type of category-value pair to any markable (node or edge).

Such 'element annotations', which describe properties of constituents, can be restricted by dictionaries of attribute-value pairs. For example, we may want to annotate the tense and aspect categories of the main predicate in the scope of a modal (or negator), we might be interested in the person and number specifications of the subject, we may want to know what type of modality is expressed in each case, etc.

As has been pointed out, element annotations are created with the `a`-command, followed by the markable and attribute-value pairs. For example, if we want to indicate that a predicate is in the simple (rather than the progressive) aspect, we can specify this for node `n5` in Figure 6 as follows:

(6) `a n5 asp:simple`

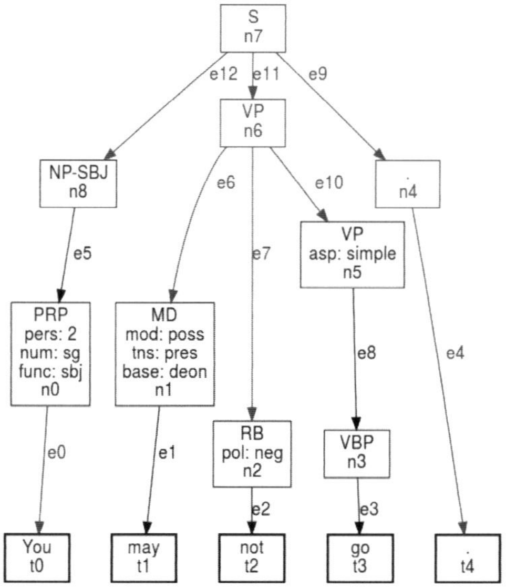

Figure 6: Element annotations

Annotations concerning tense and aspect, the grammatical categories of the subject, etc. are potentially interesting for statistical analyses, as they may correlate with specific properties of modals (e.g. their readings) and specific scope configurations. Element annotations may be useful for other purposes as well. As we will see in Section 5, identifying specific scope configurations on the basis of purely structural information – as in Figure 5 above – is possible but comes with certain disadvantages. It will therefore be beneficial to create annotations which represent sentence semantic properties and configurations more directly. Ideally, such annotations should be created automatically from a certain point onwards. For a start, we need a manually annotated corpus. As has been mentioned, we can use any type of annotation scheme, e.g. the ones proposed by Hendrickx et al. (2012), Nissim et al. (2013) and Rubinstein et al. (2013), or the (much simpler) scheme used for the annotation of the BioScope corpus (Vincze et al. 2008). In the following discussion, we will not commit ourselves to any specific annotation scheme and use generic category labels. The focus is on the process of annotation, as well as the retrievability of the annotations (cf. Section 5).

One way of adding explicit scope information is by regarding the 'higher' nodes – the *t*-nodes in Figure 5 above – as 'projections' of the relevant operators, like the `xcope`-elements in the BioScope corpus (cf. Vincze et al. 2008). Let us assume that each scope-bearing operator projects a node of category 'Op', which is located at a position in the graph that corresponds to its scope domain. This projection is, obviously, located at the semantic level (though generative grammar has long assumed 'LF-movement' for syntax-semantic mismatches, regarding it as a syntactic operation). Let us furthermore assume that each 'Op'-node comes with a specification for a 'dimension'. For the study of modals, two dimensions are particularly interesting, i.e., 'modality' and 'polarity'. Operator projections of scope-bearing elements will thus carry annotations of the type shown in (7).

(7)
```
a n7 dim:mod
a n6 dim:pol
```

The dimension of the operator node is represented as an attribute of the daughter node. For instance, if an operator node has the dimensional value 'pol(arity)', its daughter node will have an attribute-value pair of the form `pol:pos` or `pol:neg`. Such 'structural-semantic' annotations introduce additional information into the graph and facilitate search procedures considerably, as we will see in Section 5. Figure 7 shows the f(s)-layer of the graph corresponding to *You may not go.*

4.3 Representing ambiguities

Given that GraphAnno is a multi-level annotation tool, representing ambiguities is no issue at all. As has been pointed out, the number of levels is theoretically infinite. We can thus use different annotation levels for alternative readings of a given sentence. Let us reconsider (2) above. The BioScope annotators have analysed the sentence in such a way that the modal takes scope over the negation. While our knowledge of medicine is not sufficient to take a clear stance in this matter, the other reading, with the negator taking scope over the modal, actually seems more likely to us. Figure 8 shows the sentence with the two alternative readings, represented at different levels (say, 'sem1' and 'sem2') and, hence, distinguished by colours (`e8` and `e10` are green, `e9` and `e11` blue) and, in the data structure, by different values for the layer-parameters. (Note that in the graph shown in Figure 8, the identifiers linking a given scope domain to a cue have been removed, as scope dependencies are indicated with edges.)

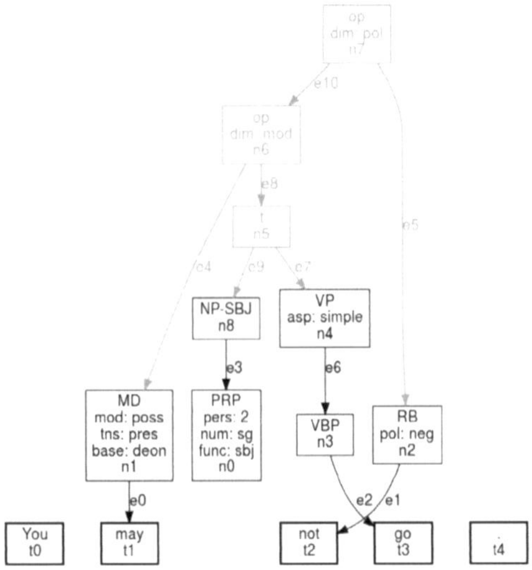

Figure 7: Annotated operator projections

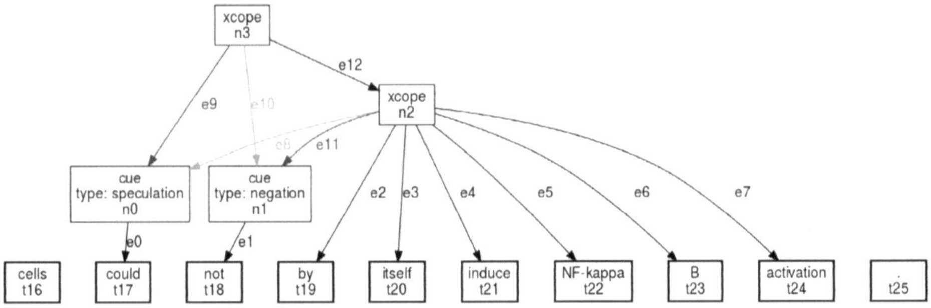

Figure 8: Scope ambiguity in GraphAnno

Importantly, the alternative scope construals can be distinguished in the query (cf. Section 5), and users can search for specific scope configurations, as well as leaving relative scope relations unspecified.

5 Searching the corpus

5.1 The query language

GraphAnno has a powerful yet transparent query language. To search for tree fragments in the corpus, the search window is opened with F7. The user specifies a graph fragment by describing it in terms of attribute-value pairs associated with nodes, as well as links between nodes. The simplest case is a text search. For instance, one can search for the modal *may* with `text may`. The hits are represented in red colour in the graph, as well as in the text line underneath.

To search for nodes with specific properties, the declaration `node` (for a single node in the graph) or `nodes` (for a set of nodes), followed by the relevant attribute-value pairs, is used in the query. For example, `node asp:simple` will find all nodes with this attribute. The same syntax can be used for edges, e.g. `edge func:pred`. The query allows regular expressions and common types of logical connectives. The following example illustrates the query 'find all nodes of category 'S' or 'VP' that are not tokens':

(8) `node cat:S|VP & !token`

For more complex tree fragments, searches for nodes and edges can be combined. The declaration `link` is used to indicate that two nodes are linked by an edge (with `edge`), or a series of edges (with `edge+`). For single-edge links, we can also just use `edge` instead of `link...edge`. To search for linked nodes, the nodes are described first and assigned a label. Node labels carry a `@`-prefix, as illustrated in (9), where two nodes are defined: `@a` (of category 'VP'), and `@b` (of category 'RB', i.e., 'adverbial', in the Penn Treebank tagset). Finally, a statement is added saying that node `@a` and node `@b` are linked by an edge.

(9)
```
node @a   cat:VP
node @b   cat:RB
edge @a@b
```

5.2 Retrieving (properties of) modals

The query language of GraphAnno offers more possibilities than pointed out above, but we will now focus on matters concerning modality. In Section 4, it was mentioned that we can identify scope configurations on the basis of purely structural information, but that it is more convenient to have a more richly annotated corpus. Let us first consider how we can retrieve specific configurations without recurring to higher-level element annotations, i.e., from a structure of the type shown in Figure 5.

To find a modal in the scope of *not*, we have to search for a node of type `t` (defined in 10a) which dominates a modal (identified in 10b) while not dominating a negation. The first of these conditions can be expressed with the statement in (10c), referring back to the nodes defined in (10a) and (10b). The second condition can be implemented using a `cond`-statement as shown in (10d). It specifies a condition saying that the set of nodes dominated by `@p` must not contain a node with the annotation 'token:not'.

(10)
```
a. node @p   cat:t
b. node @m   cat:MD
c. link @p@m edge+
d. cond @p.nodes('edge+', 'token:not').empty?
```

As for the more richly annotated structures, we have proposed to regard the top-level semantic nodes as projections of scope-bearing operators which are specified for a dimension, which in turn is represented as an attribute (with a value) on the daughter node, e.g. [`dim:pol` [`pol:neg`]]. Accordingly, we need three pieces of information in order to retrieve cooccurring scope-bearing operators. If we want to find a negator in the scope of a modal, we have to identify (i) a linked (ordered) pair of a modal operator projection and a polarity operator projection, (ii) a linked pair of a modal operator projection and a daughter node (with an attribute matching the dimensional value of its parent node), and (iii) a linked pair of a polarity projection node and a daughter node specified as a negator. Each such pair consists of a description of the two nodes in question and a `link`-statement. (11) shows how this query can be formulated in the GraphAnno query language.

(11)
```
a. node @mop      dim:mod  # modal operator (projection)
   node @nop      dim:pol  # negation (projection)
   edge @mop@nop           # direct link from modal to negation op.
b. node @mod      mod:poss # possibility modal
   edge @mop@mod           # direct link from modal proj. to modal
c. node @neg      pol:neg  # negation operator
   edge @nop@neg           # link from neg. op. (proj.) to negation
```

For the inverse scope configuration, we only have to change the order of `@mop` and `@nop` in the third line of (11a). Figure 9 shows the result of the query in (11), carried out on our mini corpus.

6 Data export

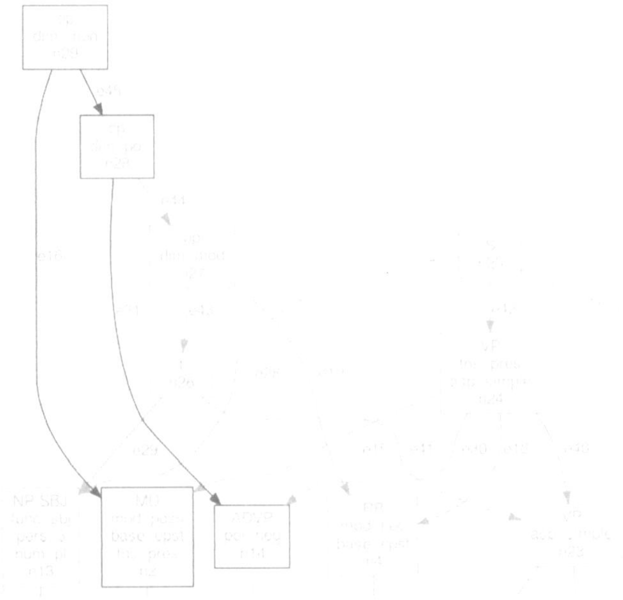

Figure 9: Displaying the result of (11) graphically

Displaying search results visually, as illustrated in Figure 9, is a good way for manually inspecting corpora. What is more important in small- and mid-scale corpus studies, however, is the possibility of exporting data sets. GraphAnno has two export options. First, it allows users to export a subcorpus meeting the conditions specified in a query, i.e., a subset of sentences meeting the relevant conditions. For instance, with the type of query illustrated above, one could compile a subcorpus containing only examples in which a modal is in the scope of negation, or vice versa. The second type of data export creates a table for quantitative analysis.

Let us assume that we want to extract annotations for sentences in which modals and negation show scope interactions, and that we are interested in the following variables:

(12) a. the tense of the main predicate in the scope of the operator
b. the aspect of the highest VP in the scope of the operator
c. the modal base (in the sense of Kratzer 1977)[13]
d. the person and number of the subject

In a first step, we have to identify the nodes carrying the information in question, just like in a search query. We can use the statement in (11) for this purpose. In addition, we have to identify the nodes carrying the temporal and aspectual information, and the subject node. We also need to specify some intermediate nodes (such as the node standing for the inner proposition, *t*), as the data export (unlike a simple query) requires a coherent graph fragment. The following set of nodes or linked pairs, in combination with (11) above, will give us the desired results:

(13)
```
node @prop      cat:t          # inner propositional node
link @mop@prop  edge+          # link from modal op. to prop. node
link @nop@prop  edge+          # link from neg. operator to prop.
node @vp        cat:VP         # VP-node
link @prop@vp   edge           # link from prop. to vp
node @sbj       cat:/.*-SBJ/   # subject node
link @prop@sbj  edge           # link from prop. node to subj
```

We can now define columns for the table to be exported with `col`, followed by the column's name and the annotation in question, in the format `@node['annotation']`, as shown in (14).

(14)
```
col mod      @mod['mod']
col base     @mod['base']
col tns      @vp['tns']
col asp      @vp['asp']
col sbj-pers @sbj['pers']
col sbj-num  @sbj['num']
```

[13] Strictly speaking, 'deontic' is not a modal base; deontic modals have a circumstantial base, and deontic is one type of ordering source. We will disregard this differentiation here, though it could easily be implemented.

7 Outlook

GraphAnno provides functionalities for a complete workflow from corpus import to data export and has been used in a number of annotation projects. With its command line interface, data input is fast, and its search and filter facilities allow users to inspect the (inevitably complex) data structures of multi-level annotation projects with reasonable ease. Even so, manual annotations are time-consuming, and automating them would represent a major step ahead in the corpus-based study of modals. It is our intention to use multi-level corpora that have been annotated with GraphAnno as an input to machine learning techniques in the near future, ultimately hoping to be able to automatically enrich existing corpus resources (like the BioScope corpus and the Penn Treebank) with additional layers of annotation.

References

Druskat, S., L. Bierkandt, V. Gast, C. Rzymski, and F. Zipser (2014). Atomic: An open-source software platform for multi-level corpus annotation. In J. Ruppert and G. Faaß (Eds.), *Proceedings of the 12th Konferenz zur Verarbeitung natrlicher Sprache (KONVENS 2014), October 2014*, pp. 228–234.

Gast, V. (2015). On the use of translation corpora in contrastive linguistics: A case study of impersonalization in english and german. *Languages in Contrast 15*(1), 4–33.

Hendrickx, I., A. Mendes, and S. Mencarelli (2012). Modality in text: A proposal for corpus annotation. In N. C. C. Chair), K. Choukri, T. Declerck, M. U. Doan, B. Maegaard, J. Mariani, A. Moreno, J. Odijk, and S. Piperidis (Eds.), *Proceedings of the 8th International Conference on Language Resources and Evaluation (LREC '12)*, Istanbul, Turkey. European Language Resources Association (ELRA).

Kratzer, A. (1977). What 'must' and 'can' must and can mean. *Linguistics & Philosophy 1*(3), 337–356.

Nissim, M., P. Pietrandrea, A. Sanso, and C. Mauri (2013). Cross-linguistic annotation of modality: A data-driven hierarchical model. In *Proceedings of the 9th Joint ISO-ACL SIGSEM Workshop on Interoperable Semantic Annotation*, Potsdam, pp. 7–14. Association for Computational Linguistics.

Rubinstein, A., H. Harner, E. Krawczyk, D. Simonson, G. Katz, and P. Portner (2013). Toward fine-grained annotation of modality in text. In *Proceedings of IWCS 2013 Workshop on Annotation of Modal Meanings in Natural Language (WAMM)*, Potsdam, Germany, pp. 38–46. Association for Computational Linguistics.

Russell, B. (1908). Mathematical logic as based on the theory of types. *American Journal of Mathematics 30*, 222–262.

Vincze, V., G. Szarvas, R. Farkas, G. Móra, and J. Csirik (2008). The BioScope corpus: Biomedical texts annotated for uncertainty, negation and their scopes. *BMC Bioinformatics 9*(S-11).

von Fintel, K. (2006). Modality and language. In D. Borchert (Ed.), *Encyclopaedia of Philosophy* (2nd ed.). Detroit: MacMillan.